Easy Piano

Disney's
My First Song Book
Volume 5

A TREASURY OF FAVORITE SONGS TO SING AND PLAY

The following songs are property of:
Bourne Co.
Music Publishers
5 West 37th Street
New York, NY 10018

HI-DIDDLE-DEE-DEE (AN ACTOR'S LIFE FOR ME)
WITH A SMILE AND A SONG

ISBN 978-1-4950-0880-1

Wonderland Music Company, Inc.
Walt Disney Music Company

DISTRIBUTED BY

7777 W. BLUEMOUND RD. P.O. BOX 13819 MILWAUKEE, WI 53213

Visit Hal Leonard Online at
www.halleonard.com

Contents

The Ballad of Davy Crockett

from Walt Disney's *Davy Crockett*

Words by TOM BLACKBURN
Music by GEORGE BRUNS

Born on a moun-tain top in Ten-nes-see, green-est state in the Land of the Free. Raised in the woods so's he knew ev-'ry tree, kilt him a b'ar when he was on-ly three. Da-vy, Da-vy Crock-ett, king of the wild fron-tier.

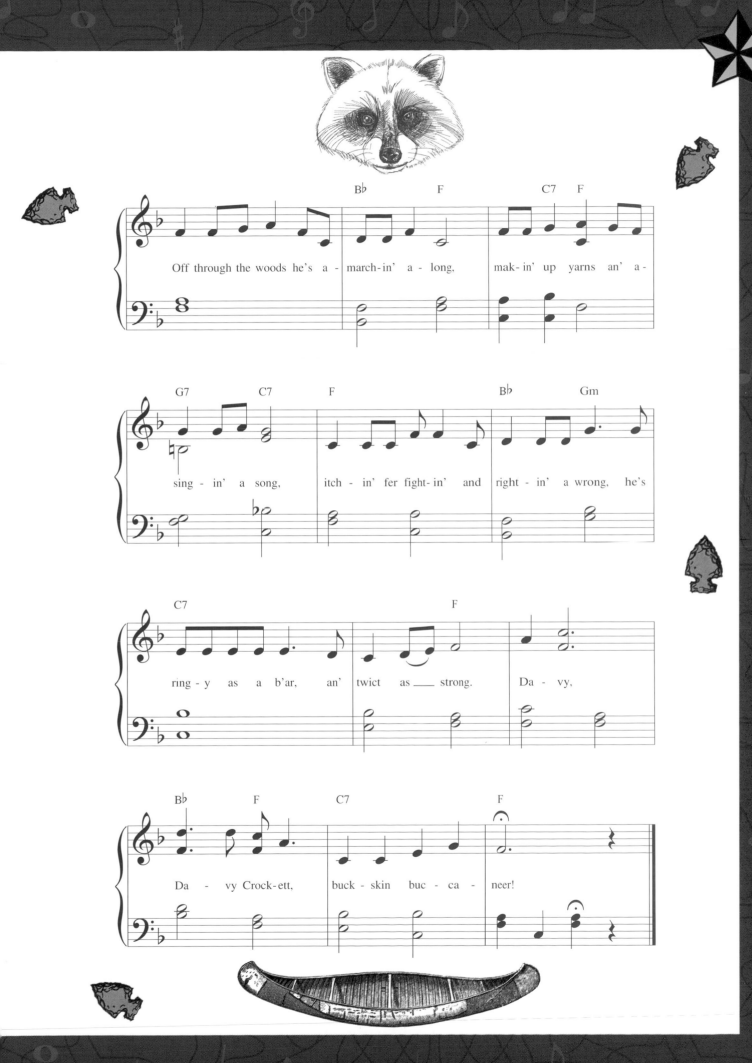

Belle

from Walt Disney's *Beauty and the Beast*

Music by ALAN MENKEN
Lyrics by HOWARD ASHMAN

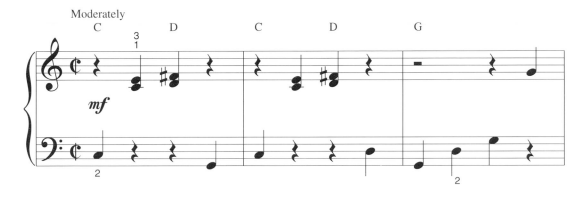

Belle: There goes the bak - er with his
Townsfolk: Look, there she goes that girl is
Townsfolk: Look, there she goes that girl is

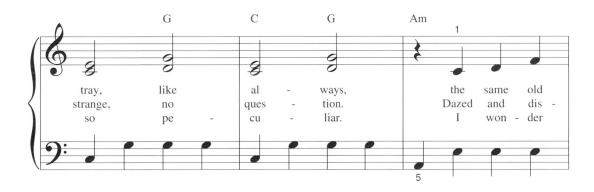

tray,   like   al - ways,   the same old
strange,   no   ques - tion.   Dazed and dis-
so   pe - cu - liar.   I won - der

G/B | C

bread and rolls to sell.
tract - ed, can't you tell?
if she's feel - ing well.

Ev - 'ry
Nev - er
With a

Eb | F | Bb | Db | Eb

morn - ing just the same
part of an - y crowd,
dream - y, far - off look

since the
'cause her
and her

morn - ing that we
head's up on some
nose stuck in a

To Coda ⊕

Ab | Fm9 | Gm7 | Abmaj7 | G7

came to this
cloud. No de -
book, what a

poor pro - vin - cial
ny - ing she's a
puz - zle to the

town.
fun - ny girl, that
rest of us is

1.
C | | Gsus

1

Dalmatian Plantation

from Walt Disney's *101 Dalmatians*

Words and Music by
MEL LEVEN

Do You Want to Build a Snowman?

from Disney's Animated Feature *Frozen*

Music and Lyrics by KRISTEN ANDERSON-LOPEZ
and ROBERT LOPEZ

LITTLE ANNA: *(Spoken:)*
Elsa? *(knocks)*

(Sung:)
Do you want to build a   snow - man?

Come on, let's go and   play!

I nev-er see you

C/E   Em   Dm

an - y - more.   Come out the   door!   It's like you've gone a - way.

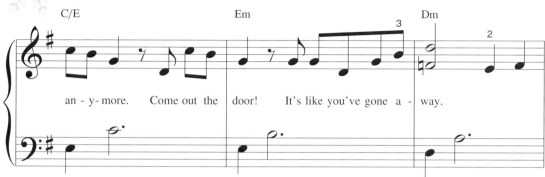

G/B   C   Bm

We used to be best   bud - dies,   and   now we're not. ___   I

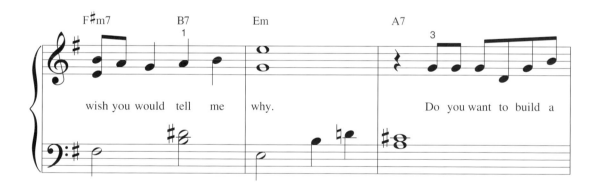

F#m7   B7   Em   A7

wish you would tell   me   why.   Do you want to build a

Am   Cm6/E♭

snow - man?   It does-n't have to be a   snow - man.

LITTLE ELSA: *(Spoken:)*
Go away, Anna.

LITTLE ANNA: *(Sung:)*
O - kay,   bye.

(knocking)

YOUNG ANNA:
Do you want to build a
mf

G

snow-man? Or ride our bike a-round the halls?

D/F#

C/E Em

I think some com-pan-y is o-ver-due; I've start-ed talk-ing to the pic-tures on the

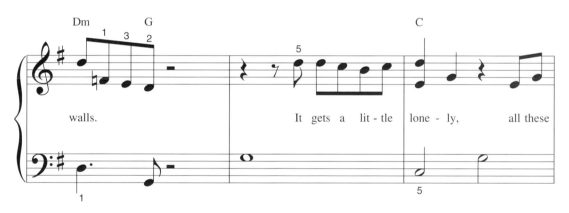

Dm G C

walls. It gets a lit-tle lone-ly, all these

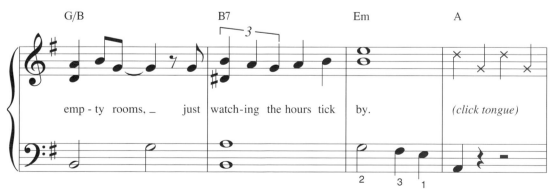

G/B B7 Em A

emp-ty rooms, _ just watch-ing the hours tick by. (click tongue)

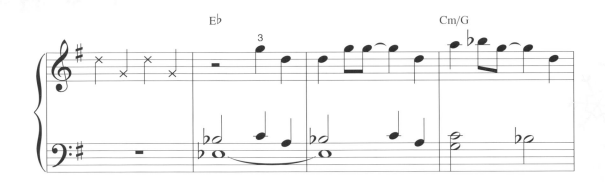

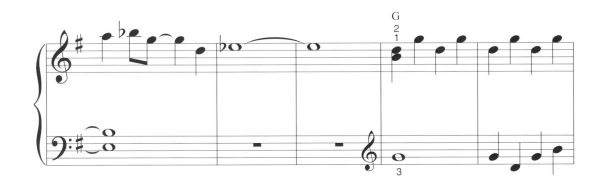

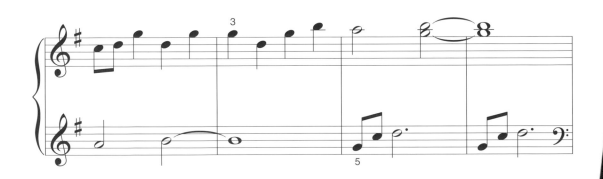

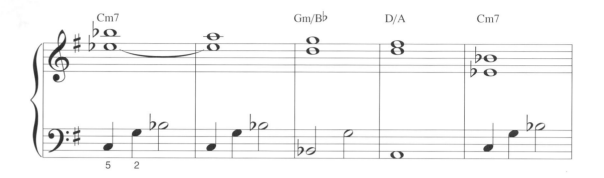

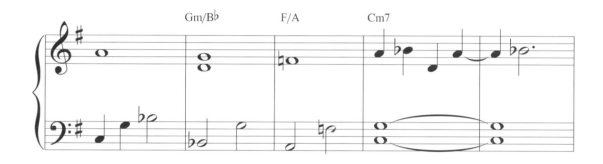

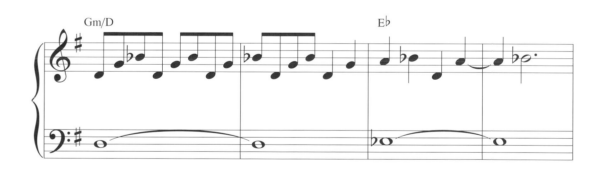

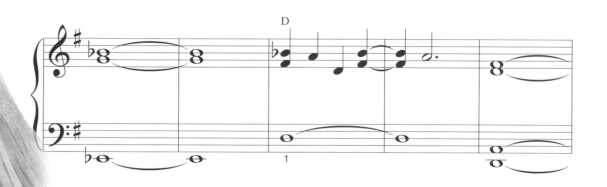

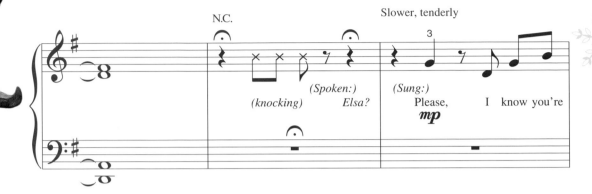

(knocking) *(Spoken:)* Elsa? *(Sung:)* Please, I know you're

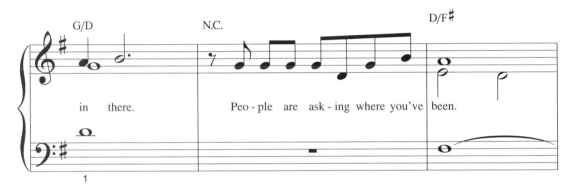

in there. Peo - ple are ask - ing where you've been.

They say, "Have cour-age," and I'm try-ing to; I'm right out here for you, just let me

in. We on - ly have each oth - er; it's just

you   and   me. ___ What are we gon - na   do?

Do you want to build a   snow-man?

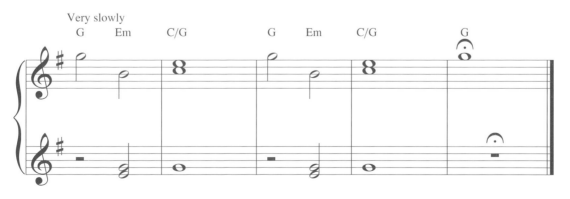

FROZEN

He's a Tramp

from Walt Disney's *Lady and the Tramp*

Words and Music by PEGGY LEE
and SONNY BURKE

tramp,   he's a   scoun-drel,   he's a   round-er,   he's a

cad.   He's a   tramp,   but I   love him.   Yes,

e - ven I have got it pret-ty   bad.   You can   nev-er tell   when

mp

he'll show up.   He gives you plen-ty of   trou - ble.

Hi-Diddle-Dee-Dee (An Actor's Life for Me)

from Walt Disney's *Pinocchio*

Words by NED WASHINGTON
Music by LEIGH HARLINE

I JUST CAN'T WAIT TO BE KING

from Walt Disney Pictures' *The Lion King*

Music by ELTON JOHN
Lyrics by TIM RICE

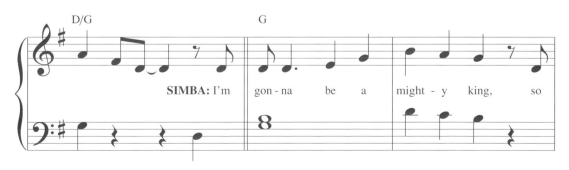

SIMBA: I'm gon-na be a might-y king, so

ZAZU: en - e - mies be - ware! Well, I've nev - er seen a king of beasts with

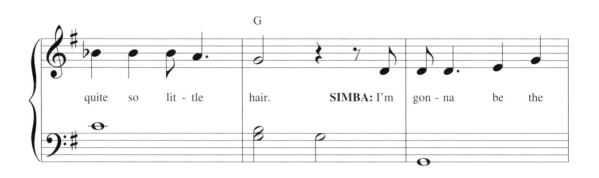

quite so lit - tle hair. **SIMBA:** I'm gon - na be the

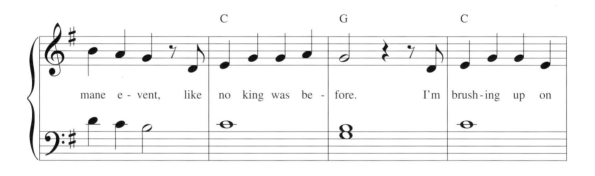

mane e - vent, like no king was be - fore. I'm brush-ing up on

look-ing down. I'm work-ing on my roar! **ZAZU:** Thus far, a rath - er

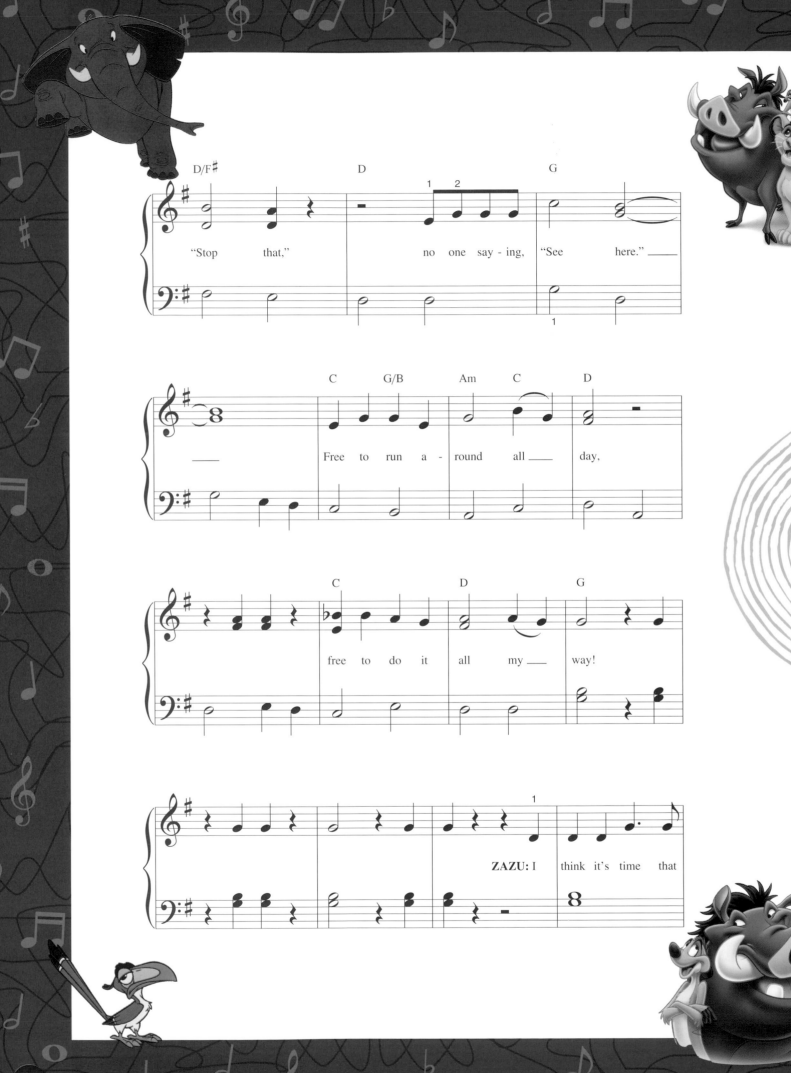

you and I   ar - ranged a   heart - to - heart.   **SIMBA:** Kings don't need ad -

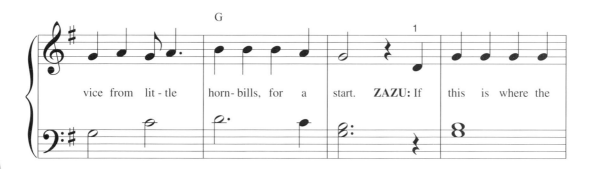

vice from lit - tle   horn - bills, for a   start.   **ZAZU:** If   this   is   where the

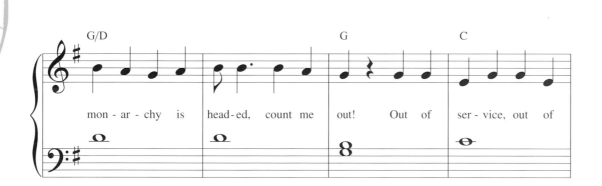

mon - ar - chy is   head - ed, count me   out!   Out   of   ser - vice, out of

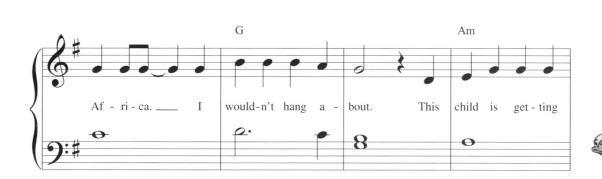

Af - ri - ca. ___   I   would-n't hang a - bout.   This   child is   get - ting

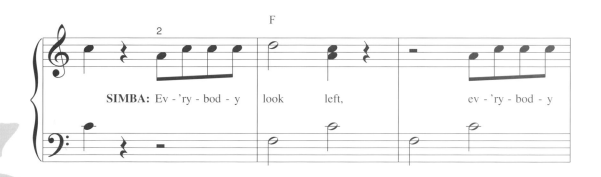

SIMBA: Ev - 'ry - bod - y   look   left,   ev - 'ry - bod - y

look   right.   Ev - 'ry - where you   look,   I'm

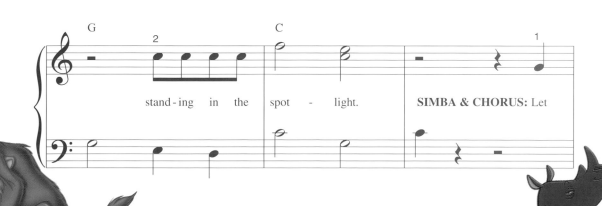

stand - ing   in   the   spot - light.   SIMBA & CHORUS: Let

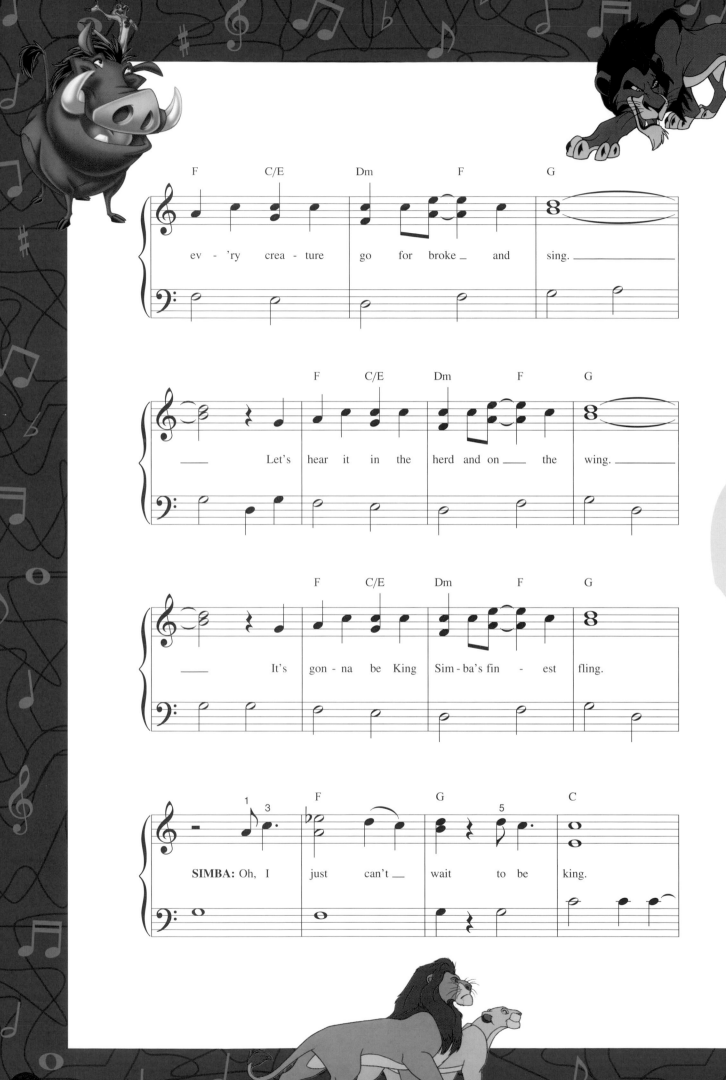

If I Didn't Have You

Walt Disney Pictures Presents A Pixar Animation Studios Film
Monsters, Inc.

Music and Lyrics by
RANDY NEWMAN

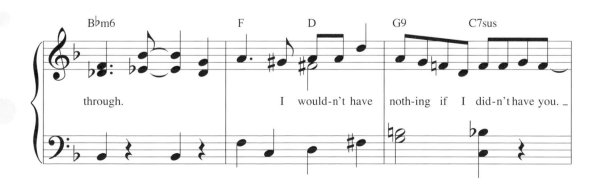

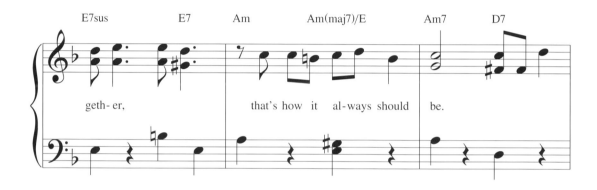

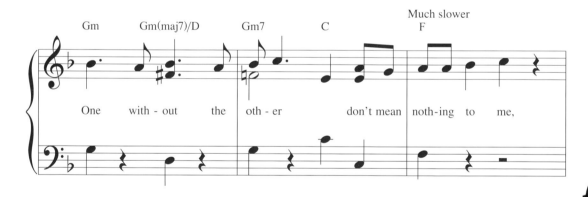

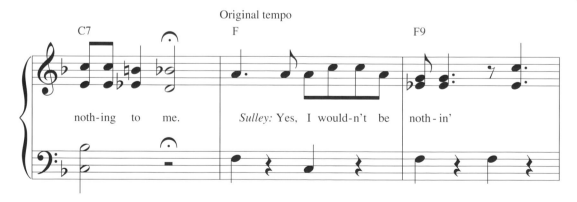

B♭6　　　　　　　　　B♭m6　　　　　　　F

if　I　did-n't have you ＿
　　　　　　　　Mike: I know what you mean,

Sulley:
I　would-n't know where to
Sulley, because...

D7　　　　　　　　G9　　　　　　　　C

go,　　　　would-n't　know　　　what to　do.
Mike: Me too, because I...　　　　　*Mike: Why do you keep singing my part?*

F　　　　　　　　F9　　　　　　　B♭6

Both: I　don't have to　　say　it　　　　　*Both:* both know it's　true. ＿
　　　　　　　　Sulley: I'll say it anyway.　　　*Mike:* 'Cause we

B♭m6　　　　　　　　F　　D7　　　G9　　　C7sus

＿　　　　　　　　　　I　would-n't have　　noth-in' if　I　did-n't have,

45

I would-n't have noth-in' if I did-n't have, I would-n't have

Much slower

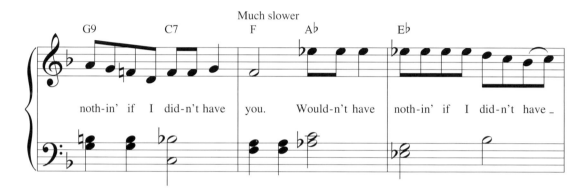

noth-in' if I did-n't have you. Would-n't have noth-in' if I did-n't have _

Original tempo

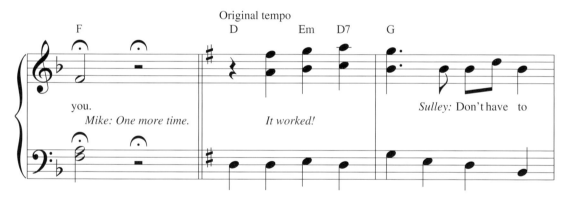

you.
Mike: One more time.   *It worked!*   *Sulley:* Don't have to

say it
Mike: Where'd everybody come from?   *Sulley:* 'cause we both know it's true. ___   *Mike:* Let's take it home, big guy!

Let It Go

from Disney's Animated Feature *Frozen*

Music and Lyrics by KRISTEN ANDERSON-LOPEZ
and ROBERT LOPEZ

Half-time feel, mysterious

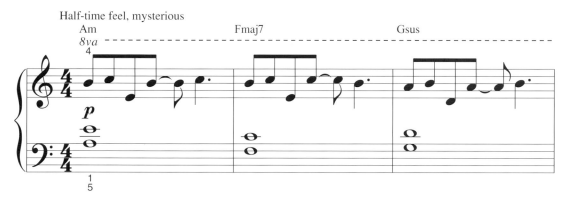

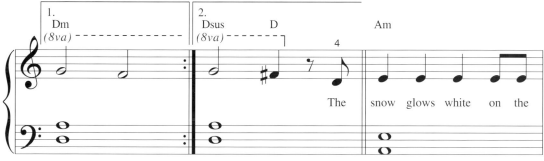

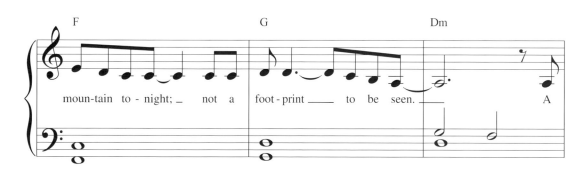

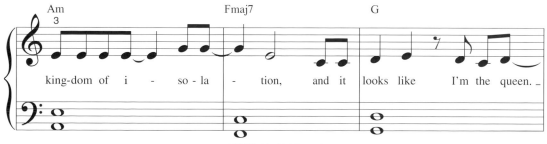

_The wind ___ is howl - ing like this_

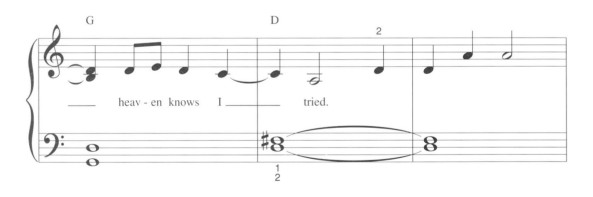

_swirl - ing storm in - side. ___ Could-n't keep it in, ____

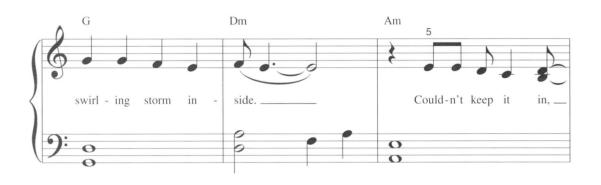

____ heav - en knows I ___ tried._

_Don't let ___ them in, don't let them see; be the good girl you_

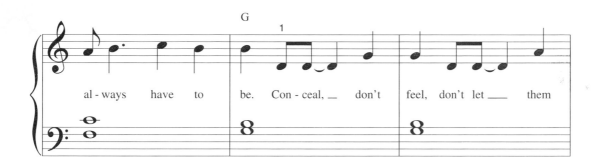

al - ways have to be. Con - ceal, __ don't feel, don't let ___ them

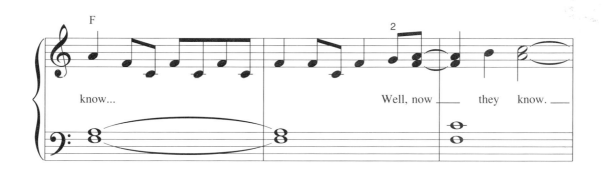

know... Well, now ___ they know. ___

Let it go, ___ let it go; ___ can't __
let it go; ___ I am

hold it back an - y - more. ___ Let it go, ___ let it go; _
one with the wind and sky. Let it go, ___ let it go; _

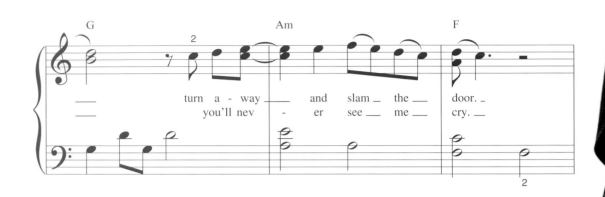

turn a - way ___ and slam ___ the ___ door.
you'll nev - er see ___ me ___ cry.

I don't ___ care ___ what they're going to ___ say; ___
Here I ___ stand, ___ and here I'll ___ stay; ___

To Coda ⊕

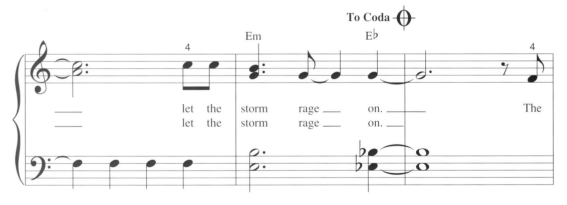

let the storm rage ___ on. ___ The
let the storm rage ___ on.

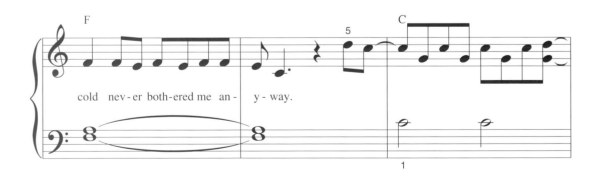

cold nev - er both - ered me an - y - way.

It's fun-ny how some dis - tance makes

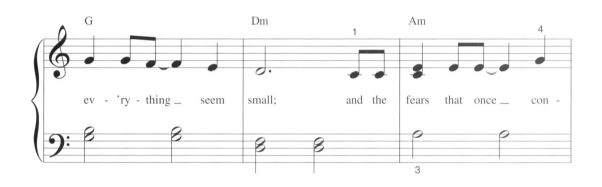

ev - 'ry - thing _ seem small; and the fears that once _ con -

trolled me can't get to me _ at all.

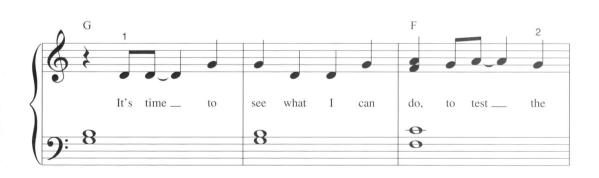

It's time _ to see what I can do, to test _ the

lim - its and break through. No right, _ no wrong, no rules for me, _

D.S. al Coda

_ I'm free! Let it go, _

CODA

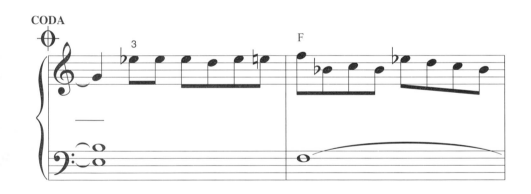

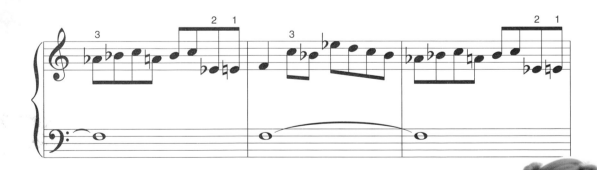

My pow – er flur – ries through the air in – to the

ground. My soul ___ is spi – ral – ing in

fro – zen frac – tals all a – round. ___ And one ___ thought

crys – tal – liz – es like an i – cy blast:

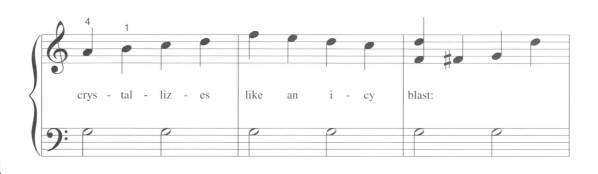

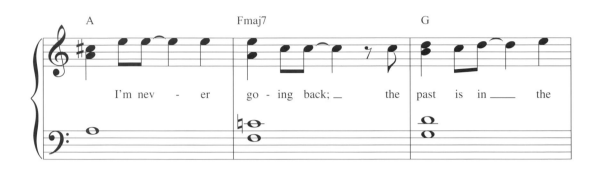

I'm nev - er   go - ing back;   the   past   is   in   the

past!   Let   it   go,   let   it   go,

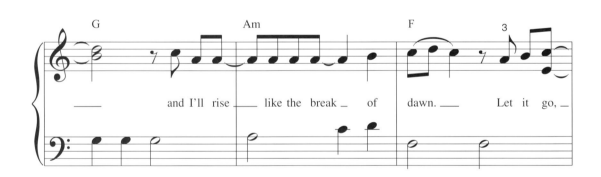

and I'll rise   like the break   of   dawn.   Let   it   go,

let   it   go;   that   per - fect   girl   is

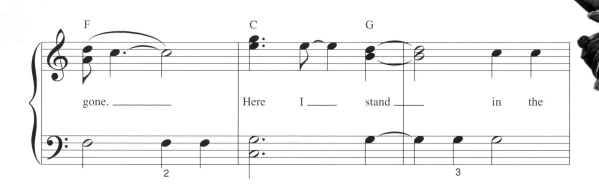

gone. _____   Here   I ____ stand ____   in the

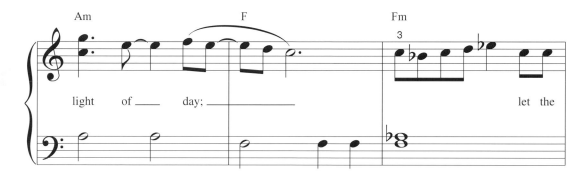

light   of ____ day; ____ _____   let the

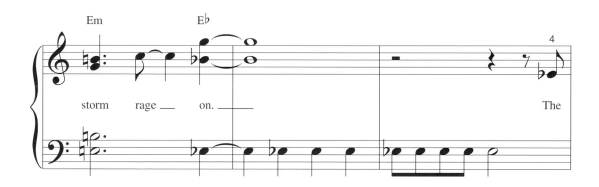

storm   rage ____ on. ____   The

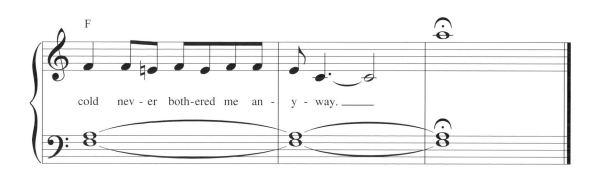

cold   nev - er both-ered me an - y - way. ____

Love Is a Song

from Walt Disney's *Bambi*

Words by LARRY MOREY
Music by FRANK CHURCHILL

Moderately

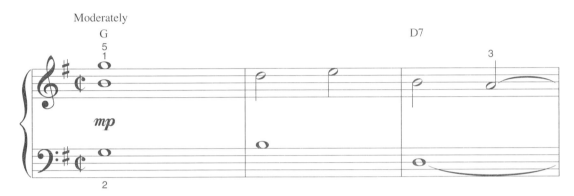

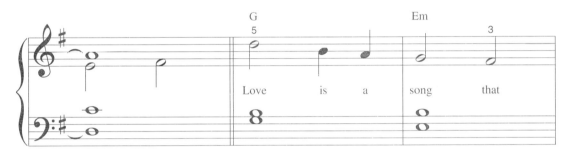

Love is a song that

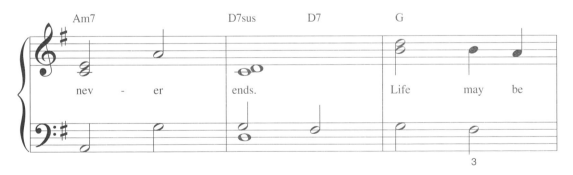

nev - er ends. Life may be

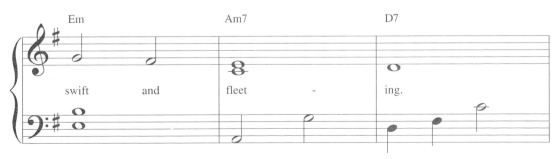

swift and fleet - ing.

Hope may die, yet love's beau - ti - ful

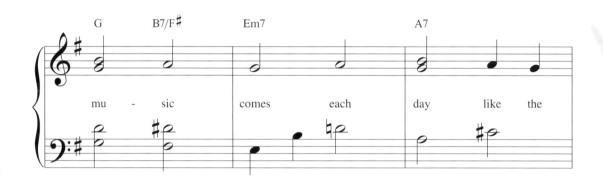

mu - sic comes each day like the

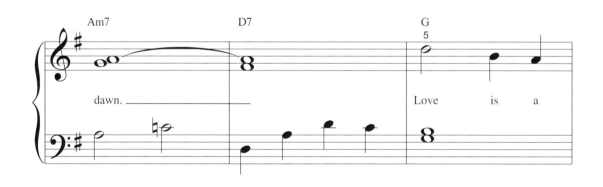

dawn. _____ Love is a

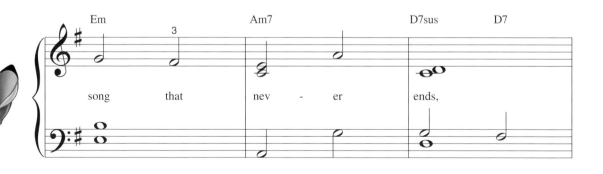

song that nev - er ends,

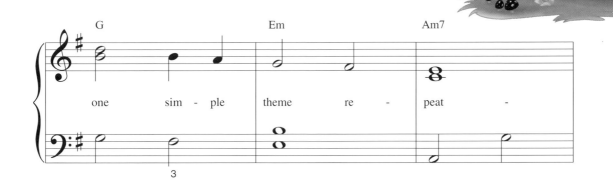

one   sim - ple   theme   re -   peat -

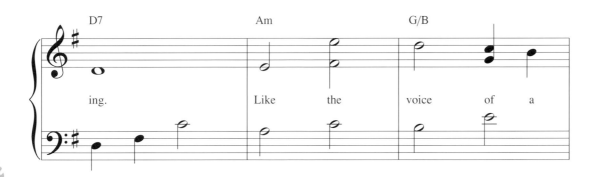

ing.   Like   the   voice   of   a

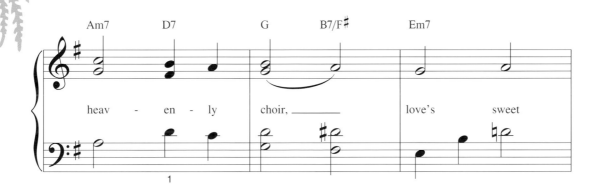

heav - en - ly   choir, _____   love's   sweet

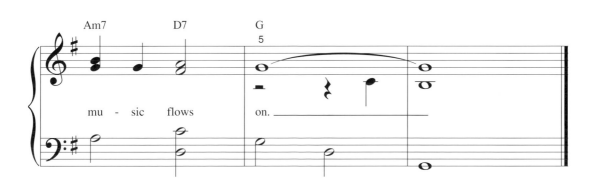

mu - sic   flows   on. _____

So Close

from Walt Disney Pictures' *Enchanted*

Music by ALAN MENKEN
Lyrics by STEPHEN SCHWARTZ

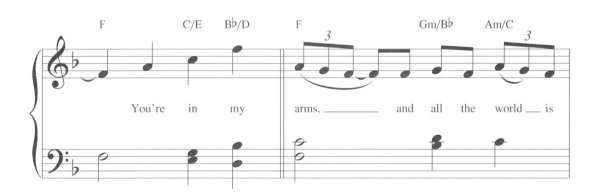

You're in my arms, and all the world is

gone, the mu- sic play- ing on for on- ly

two. So close to - geth - er;

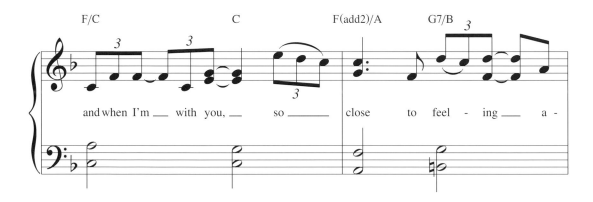

and when I'm __ with you, __ so ____ close to feel - ing __ a -

live. A life ____ goes

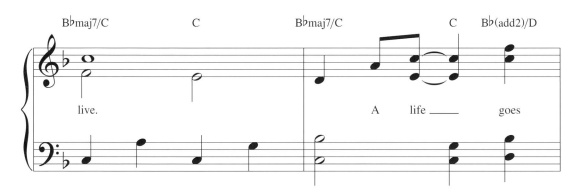

by; ro - man - tic dreams _ must die. So I bid mine good -

bye,   and nev - er ___ knew   so

close   was wait - ing, ___ wait-ing here ___ with you. ___ And ___

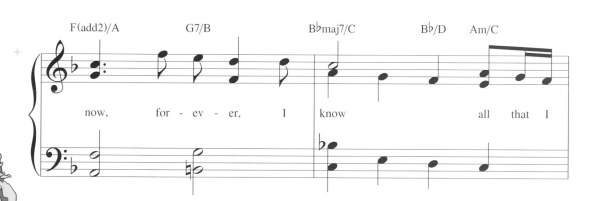

now,   for - ev - er, I know   all that I

want is ___ to hold you ___ so close.   So ___

close to reach-ing that fa-mous hap-py end, ___ al -

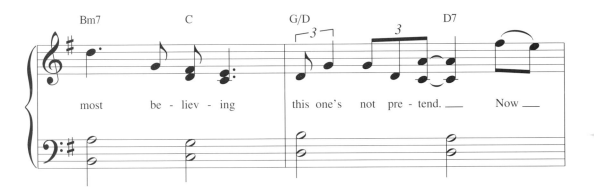

most be-liev-ing this one's not pre-tend. ___ Now ___

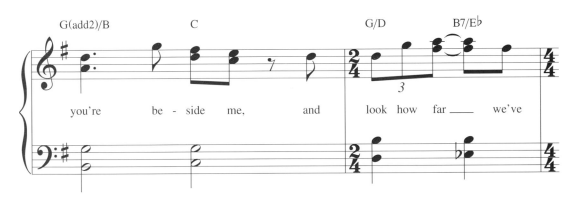

you're be-side me, and look how far ___ we've

come. So far, we ___ are so ___

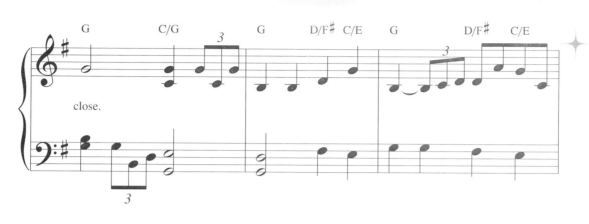

close.

Oh,

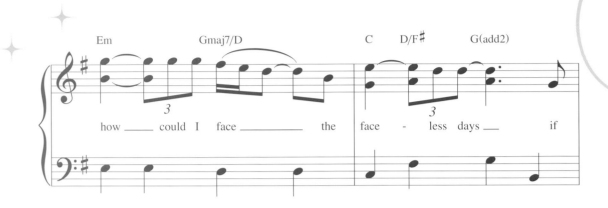

how ____ could I face _____ the face - less days ____ if

I should lose ____ you ____ now? _____

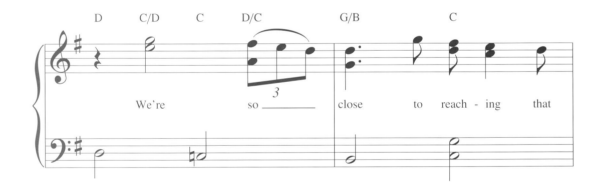

We're so _____ close to reach - ing that

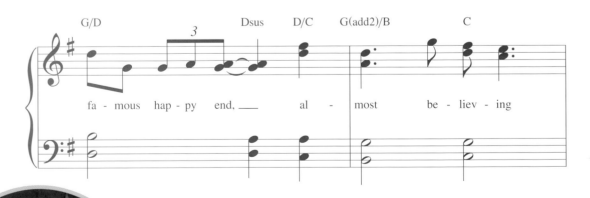

fa - mous hap - py end, ____ al - most be - liev - ing

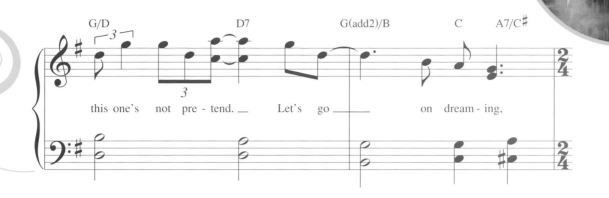

this one's not pre-tend. __ Let's go ____ on dream-ing,

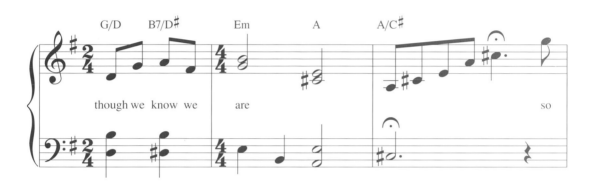

though we know we are ____ so

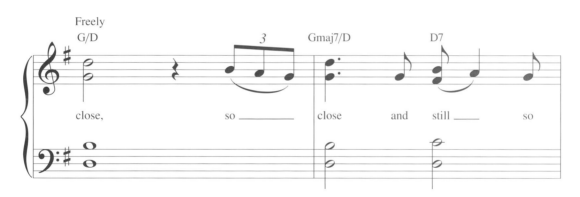

Freely

close, so ____ close and still ____ so

A tempo

far.

ENCHANTED

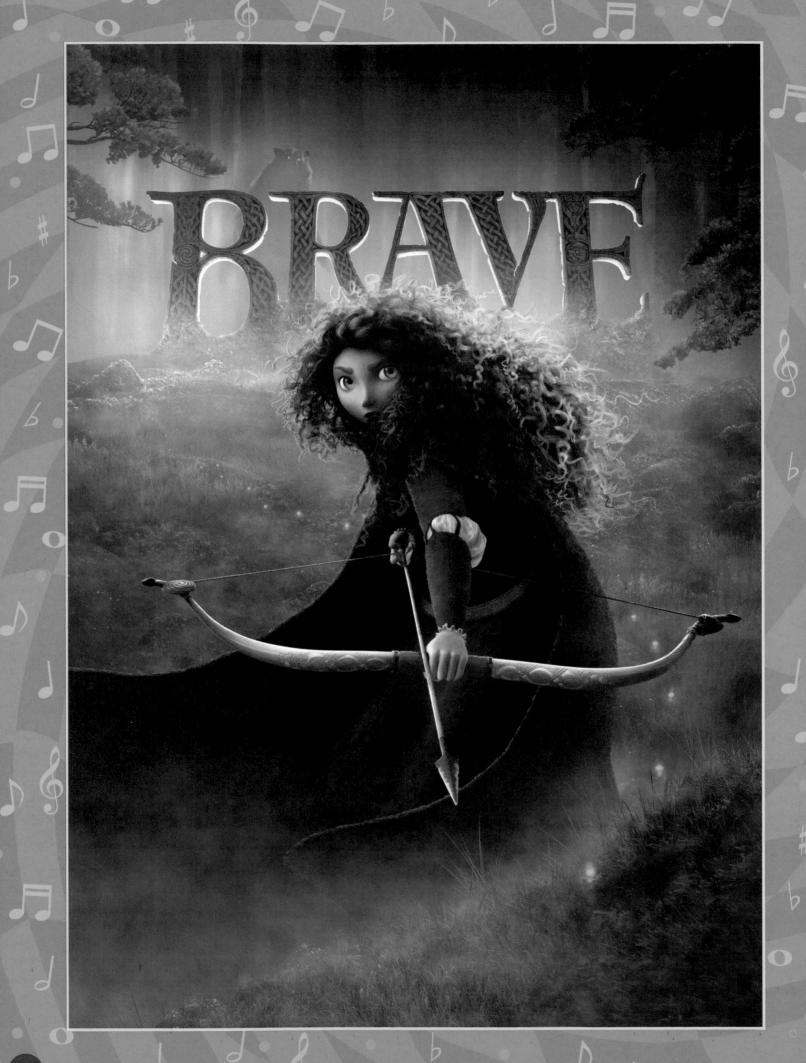

Touch the Sky

from the Walt Disney/Pixar film
Brave

Music by ALEXANDER L. MANDEL
Lyrics by ALEXANDER L. MANDEL
and MARK ANDREWS

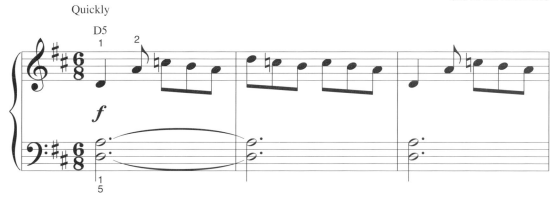

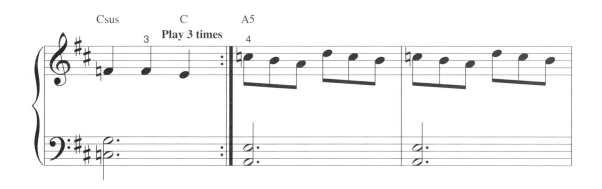

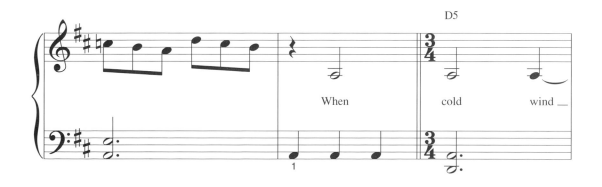

G

_____ is a call - ing, and the

D5   G

sky ___ is clear and ___ bright, mist - y

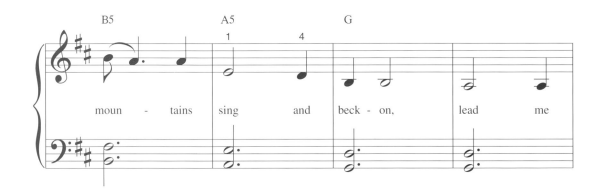

B5   A5   G

moun - tains sing and beck - on, lead me

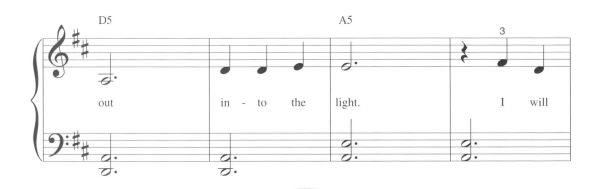

D5   A5

out in - to the light. I will

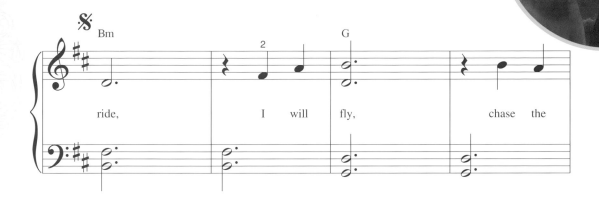

ride,   I will fly,   chase the

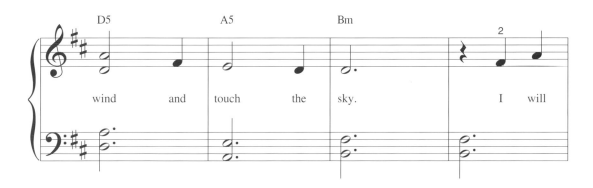

wind   and   touch   the   sky.   I will

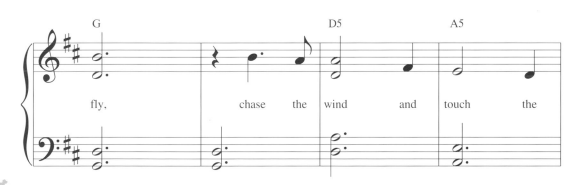

fly,   chase the   wind   and   touch   the

sky.   Na   na   na   na,   na   na

73

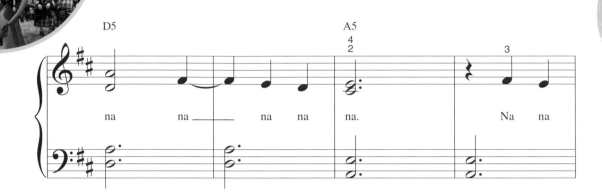

na na _____ na na na.   Na na

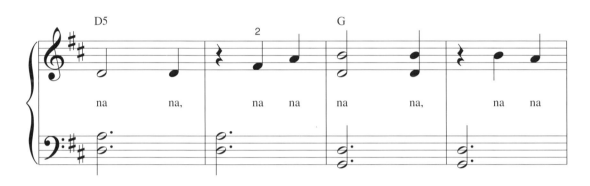

na na, na na na na, na na

To Coda $\oplus$

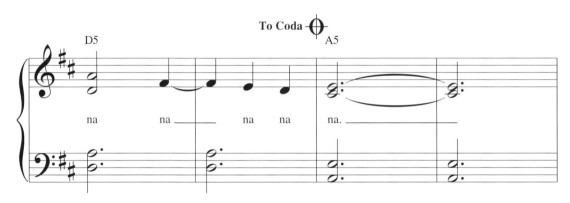

na na _____ na na na. _____

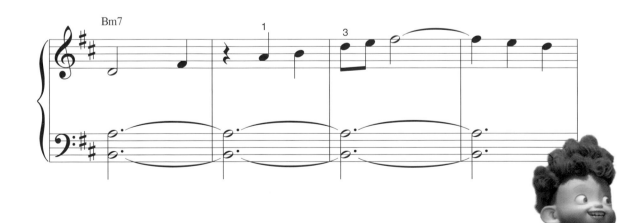

74

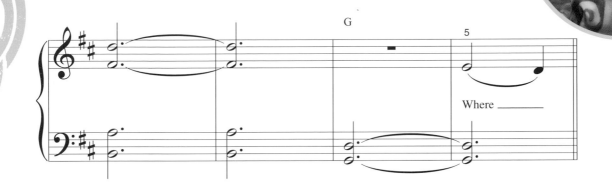

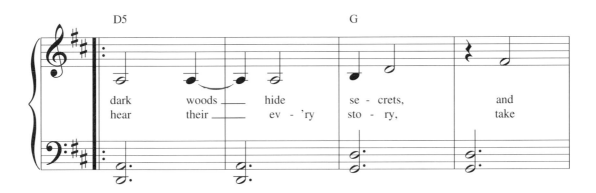

Where _____

D5   G

dark   woods _____ hide   se - crets,   and
hear   their _____ ev - 'ry   sto - ry,   take

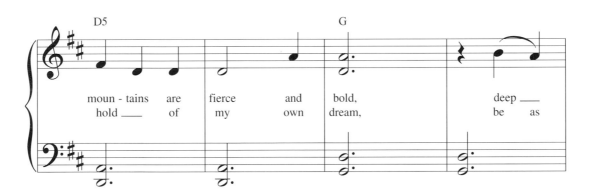

D5   G

moun - tains are   fierce   and   bold,   deep _____
hold _____ of   my   own   dream,   be as

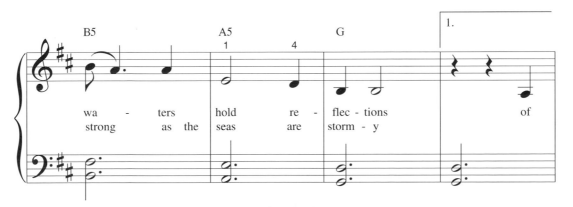

B5   A5   G   1.

wa -   ters   hold   re - flec - tions   of
strong   as the   seas   are   storm - y

D5   A5

times lost long a - go.   I will

2.   5 A5   D5

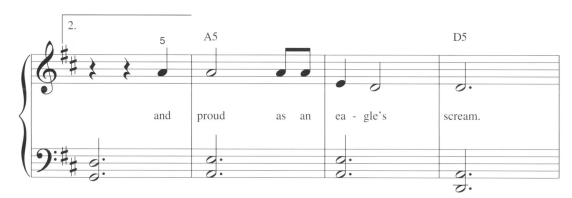

and proud as an ea - gle's scream.

D.S. al Coda

I will

CODA

A5   D5

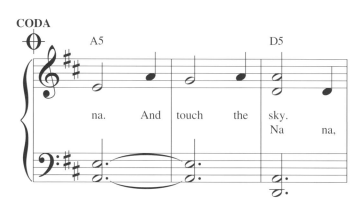

na. And touch the sky. Na na,

G   D5

na na na na, na na na na, __

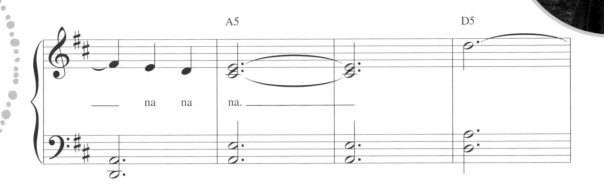

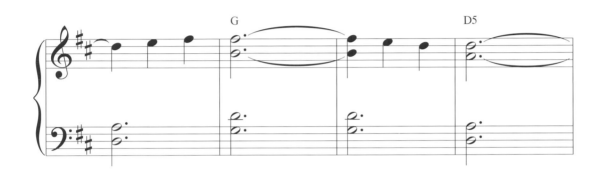

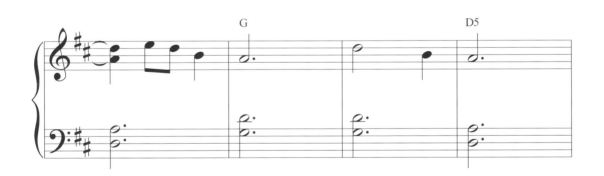

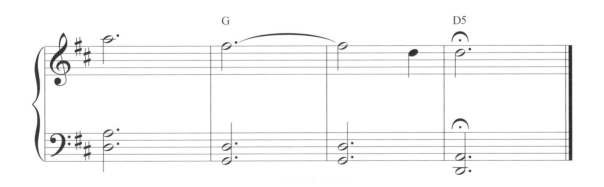

TOYLAND MARCH

from Walt Disney's
Babes in Toyland

Adapted From V. HERBERT Melody
Words by MEL LEVEN
Music by GEORGE BRUNS

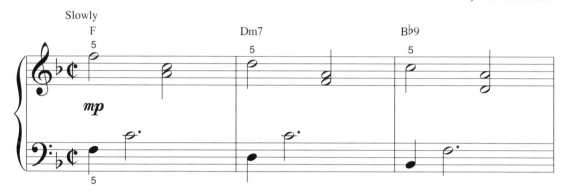

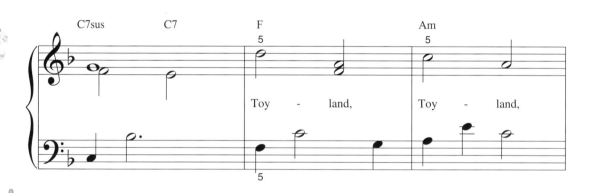

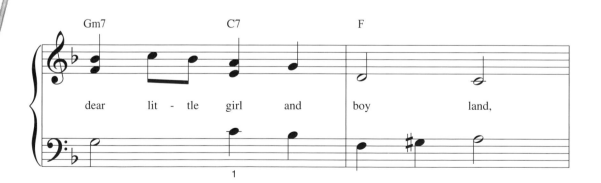

Bb   Bbm   F/C

while   you dwell   with - in   it   you are

G7   Csus   C   F

ev - er   hap - py   then.   Child - hood's

Am   Gm7   C

toy - land,   won - der - ful   world   of

F   Bb   Bbm

joy   land,   would - n't   it   be

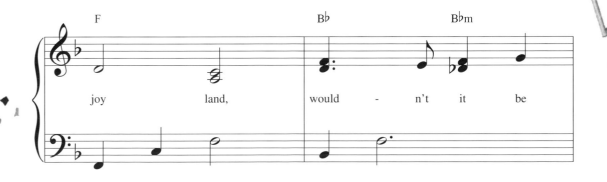

F/C   D7   Gm   C7

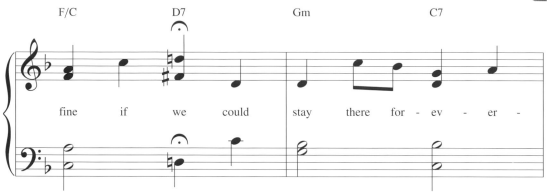

fine   if   we   could   stay   there   for - ev - er -

F   Am

more?   Toy - land,   Toy - land,

Gm7   C7   F

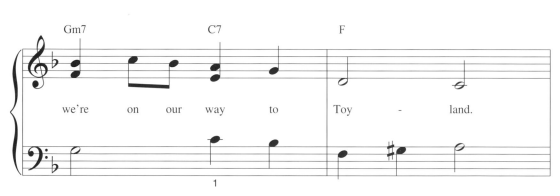

we're   on   our   way   to   Toy - land.

B♭   B♭m   F/C

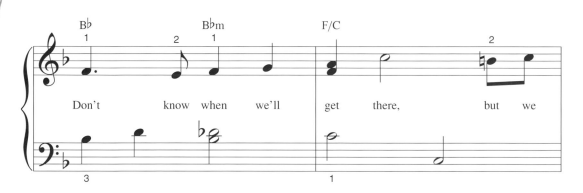

Don't   know when   we'll   get   there,   but   we

Trashin' the Camp

from Walt Disney Pictures' *Tarzan*™

Words and Music by
PHIL COLLINS

When Will My Life Begin

from Walt Disney Pictures'
Tangled

Music by ALAN MENKEN
Lyrics by GLENN SLATER

Moderately fast Rock

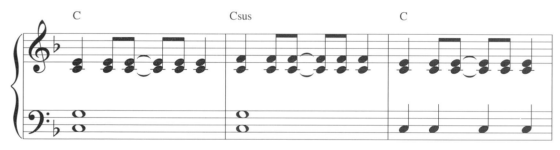

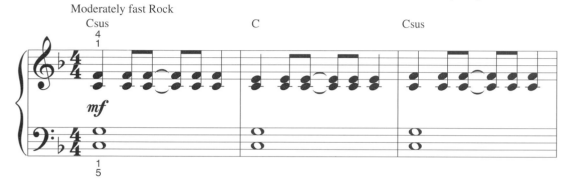

Sev - en a. m., ___ the u - su - al morn - ing
Then af - ter lunch, _ it's puz - zles, and darts and

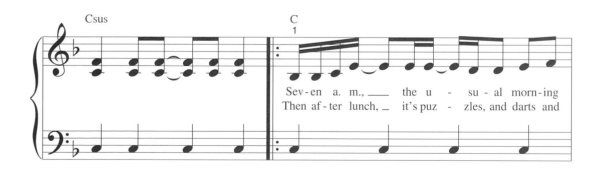

line - up. _____
bak - ing... _____

Start on the chores, _ and sweep _ 'til the floor's all
pa - per mâ - ché, _ a bit ___ of bal - let and

gal - ler - y; ____ I'll play gui - tar, and knit, __ and cook, and
room some - where. __ And then I'll brush, and brush, __ and brush, and

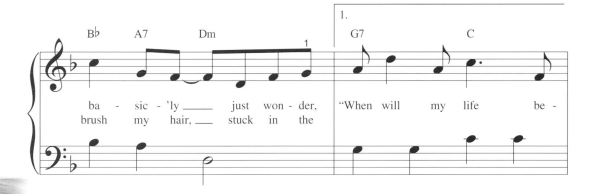

ba - sic - 'ly ____ just won - der, "When will my life be -
brush my hair, __ stuck in the

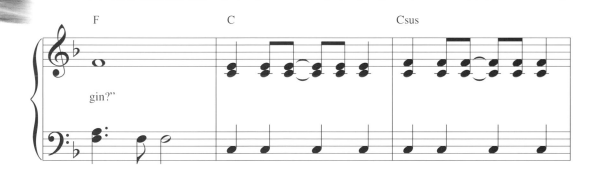

gin?"

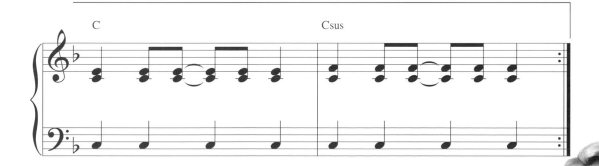

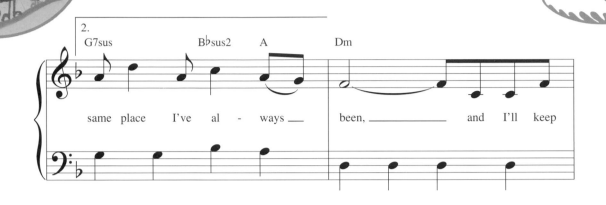

2.

G7sus   B♭sus2   A   Dm

same place   I've   al - ways ___   been, _____   and   I'll   keep

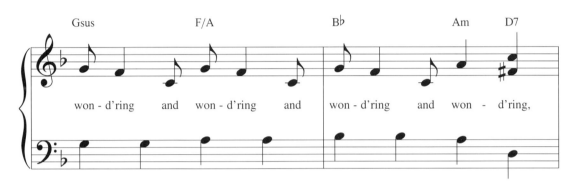

Gsus   F/A   B♭   Am   D7

won - d'ring   and   won - d'ring   and   won - d'ring   and   won - d'ring,

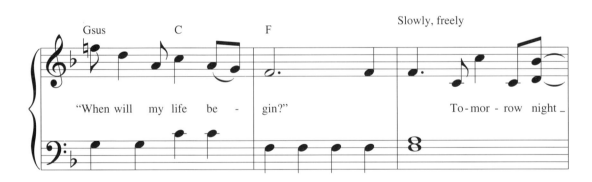

Gsus   C   F   *Slowly, freely*

"When   will   my   life   be - gin?"   To - mor - row   night ___

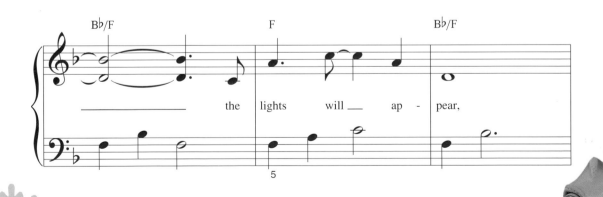

B♭/F   F   B♭/F

_____   the   lights   will ___   ap - pear,

5

just like they do on ___ my birth - day ___ each

year. What is ___ it like out

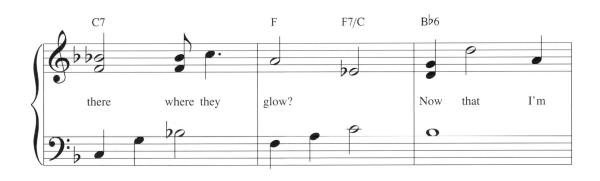

there where they glow? Now that I'm

old - er, ___ Moth - er might just ___ let me go...